CORE LIBRARY GUIDE TO RACISM IN MODERN AMERICA

JUSTICE FOR GEORGE FLOYD

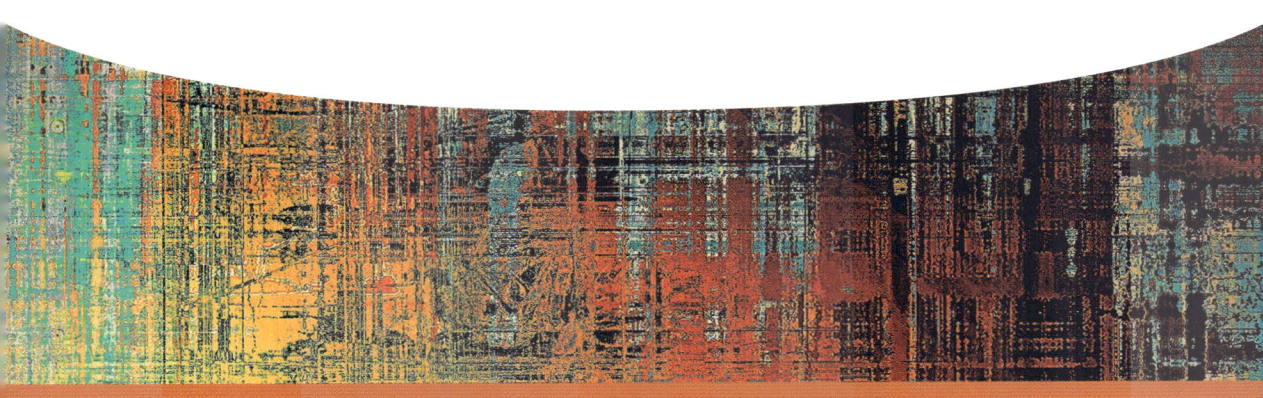

BY DUCHESS HARRIS, JD, PHD
WITH TAMMY GAGNE

Cover image: A memorial honoring George Floyd was put up outside Cup Foods in Minneapolis, Minnesota. Floyd died in police custody outside the store.

Core Library

An Imprint of Abdo Publishing
abdobooks.com

abdobooks.com

Published by Abdo Publishing, a division of ABDO, PO Box 398166, Minneapolis, Minnesota 55439. Copyright © 2021 by Abdo Consulting Group, Inc. International copyrights reserved in all countries. No part of this book may be reproduced in any form without written permission from the publisher. Core Library™ is a trademark and logo of Abdo Publishing.

Printed in the United States of America, North Mankato, Minnesota
102020
012021

Cover Photo: Jason Armond/Los Angeles Times/Getty Images
Interior Photos: Kerem Yucel/AFP/Getty Images, 4–5; Stephen Maturen/Getty Images News/Getty Images, 6; Red Line Editorial, 9, 27; Rose Baca/The Dallas Morning News/AP Images, 11; Mario Tama/Getty Images News/Getty Images, 14–15; Shutterstock Images, 17; Karla Ann Cote/NurPhoto/AP Images, 19; John Minchillo/AP Images, 20, 43; Stas Walenga/Shutterstock Images, 22; Michael Nigro/Sipa USA/AP Images, 24–25; Godofredo A. Vásquez/Houston Chronicle/AP Images, 30; Chris Tuite/ImageSPACE/MediaPunch/IPX/AP Images, 32–33; Hennepin County Sheriff's Office/AP Images, 36–37; Katie Abdo, 40

Editor: Katharine Hale
Series Designer: Sarah Taplin

Library of Congress Control Number: 2020944047

Publisher's Cataloging-in-Publication Data

Names: Harris, Duchess, author. | Gagne, Tammy, author.
Title: Justice for George Floyd / by Duchess Harris and Tammy Gagne
Description: Minneapolis, Minnesota : Abdo Publishing, 2021 | Series: Core library guide to racism in modern America | Includes online resources and index
Identifiers: ISBN 9781532194658 (lib. bdg.) | ISBN 9781644945087 (pbk.) | ISBN 9781098214173 (ebook)
Subjects: LCSH: Trials (Police misconduct)--Juvenile literature. | Police shootings--Juvenile literature. | Police brutality--United States--Juvenile literature. | United States--History--Juvenile literature. | Race relations--Juvenile literature. | Black lives matter movement--Juvenile literature.
Classification: DDC 363.232--dc23

CONTENTS

CHAPTER ONE
George Floyd, Say His Name! 4

CHAPTER TWO
I Can't Breathe 14

CHAPTER THREE
Remembering George Floyd 24

CHAPTER FOUR
A Man Who Made a Difference 32

Important Dates 42

Stop and Think 44

Glossary 45

Online Resources 46

Learn More 46

About the Authors 47

Index 48

CHAPTER ONE

GEORGE FLOYD, SAY HIS NAME!

It was May 26, 2020. People gathered at Chicago Avenue and 38th Street in Minneapolis, Minnesota. Rain fell from the sky. The COVID-19 pandemic was still raging across the United States. This deadly disease is caused by a contagious virus. Cities and states were on lockdown. People were asked to stay home. This was to help stop the virus from spreading. But neither the weather nor the pandemic stopped the protesters. They were

On May 26, 2020, protesters led a march to protest the death of George Floyd.

The Third Police Precinct in Minneapolis became the site of several protests in the days following Floyd's death.

heartbroken and furious about the death of an unarmed Black man. His name was George Floyd.

Floyd had died the day before at this location. He was in the custody of Officer Derek Chauvin. Chauvin, who is white, forced Floyd to the ground. He knelt on

Floyd's neck. Chauvin applied pressure to Floyd's neck for more than eight minutes. Floyd said he could not breathe. Three other officers were involved. Thomas Lane and J. Alexander Kueng were rookie officers. They had only recently finished their training. Tou Thao had been with the department for several years. Chauvin was a training officer. He was the most superior officer in the group. Both Lane and Kueng spoke up

PERSPECTIVES
COMPLAINTS ON FILE
Floyd's death was not the first time Chauvin's or Thao's behavior had been questioned. Both officers had numerous prior complaints. Chauvin had at least 17 complaints. These included complaints of excessive force. Thao had six complaints. He had been sued for excessive force in 2017. The Minneapolis Police Department had redacted many details in the officers' personnel files. This means information was kept private. Many people thought that neither man should have still been working as a police officer at the time of Floyd's death.

when they saw what Chauvin was doing. But none of the officers took any action to stop Chauvin.

A day later, protesters held signs with phrases such as "Black lives matter!" and "Stop killing Black people!" The group marched to the police station where the officers worked. They had been fired earlier that day. But the protesters were angry that murder charges had not been filed against the officers. The people demanded justice for the man who could no longer speak for himself.

> ### DEMANDING JUSTICE
> People continued to protest in the days following George Floyd's death. They wanted justice. Minneapolis mayor Jacob Frey was one of them. Frey held a press conference on May 27, 2020. He asked Hennepin County Attorney Mike Freeman to charge Chauvin. He insisted that Floyd, Floyd's family, and the Black community deserved justice. Chauvin was charged on May 29.

UNEQUAL NUMBERS

In 2017, 27 percent of people who were killed by police were Black, while making up just 13 percent of the US population. This chart compares the breakdown of the US population by ethnicity with fatal police shootings and police shootings of unarmed people. What do you notice about the graph? How does the graph help you understand the text?

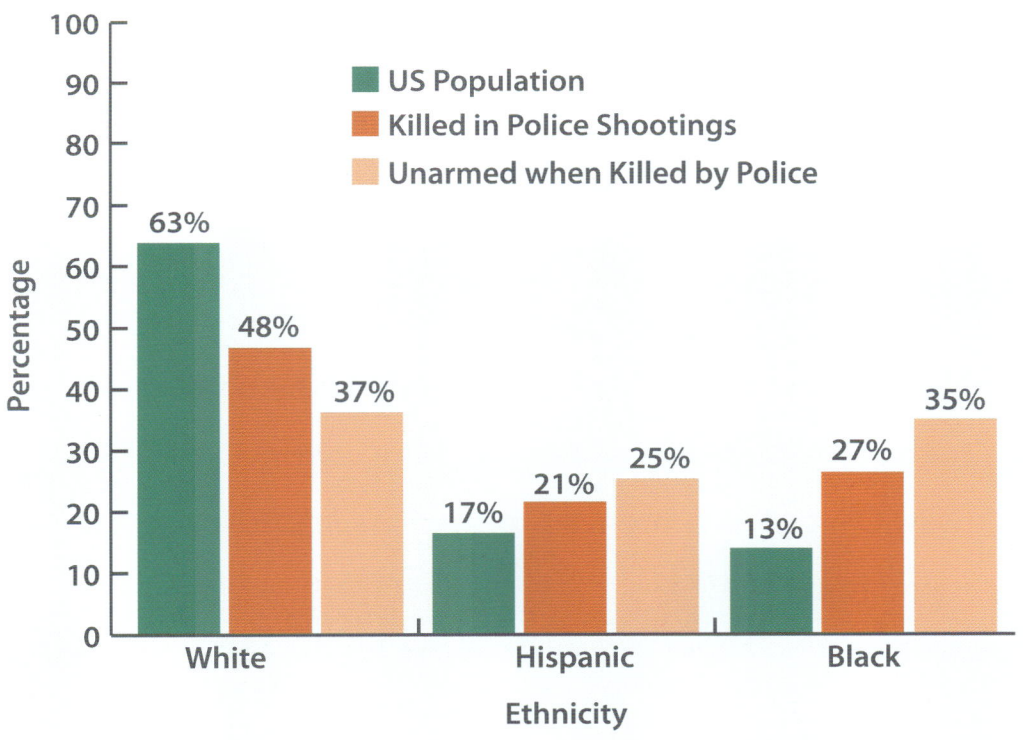

Fatal shootings of people in other ethnic groups not represented in graph.

ONE OF MANY

Floyd is one of many Black people who have died while in police custody in the United States. In 2014 Eric Garner died during an arrest in New York. Officer Daniel Pantaleo restrained Garner with a choke hold. Garner told Pantaleo that he could not breathe. But Pantaleo did not release Garner. Pantaleo was fired five years later. But he was not charged with a crime.

In 2017 a Texas police officer shot and killed 15-year-old Jordan Edwards. The unarmed Black teen was a passenger in a car. Police had come to investigate a party. Jordan and his friends were leaving the party. Officer Roy Oliver fired at the vehicle. Police originally reported that the car was driving toward the officer. But body camera footage showed the car driving away. Oliver was sentenced to 15 years in prison for the murder.

Just months before Floyd's death, Breonna Taylor slept in her bed. She was an emergency medical

Roy Oliver was found guilty of murdering Jordan Edwards. Guilty verdicts for police officers involved in shootings are rare.

technician in Louisville, Kentucky. Her boyfriend, Kenneth Walker, was with her. Walker and Taylor heard loud banging at the door. Walker says they asked who it was. But there was no answer. Then Louisville police broke down Taylor's door. They were executing a no-knock warrant in search of drugs. The main suspect was already in custody. But police thought he was receiving mail at Taylor's apartment. Walker thought they were being robbed. He fired a shot from his licensed gun. Officers Jon Mattingly, Myles Cosgrove, and Brett Hankison returned fire. Taylor died from multiple gunshot wounds. Hankison fired shots from outside the apartment. Some went into a neighboring apartment. The Louisville Police Department fired him in June. Hankison was charged with wanton endangerment in September. But none of the officers were charged for Taylor's death.

Black people face a much higher risk of being killed by police than white people do. In some parts of the United States, police kill on average 2 times more Black people than white people. In the Chicago metropolitan area, that ratio can be as high as 6.51 to 1. Experts say that systemic racism plays a big role in this problem. Racism is the mistreatment of a person because of that person's race. Systemic racism occurs when a society's systems and practices put people of a certain race at a disadvantage. Floyd became a symbol of systemic racism in the United States.

STRAIGHT TO THE
SOURCE

Former NBA player Stephen Jackson was one of Floyd's closest friends. He refers to Floyd as his twin. Jackson delivered a speech at Minneapolis City Hall on May 29, 2020. He spoke out against Chauvin's actions:

> *I'm here because they're not going to demean the character of George Floyd, my twin. A lot of times, when the police do things that they know that's wrong, the first thing they try to do is cover it up and bring up your background to make it seem like the [thing] that they did was worth it. When was murder ever worth it? But if it's a Black man, it's approved. You can't tell me when that man had his knee on my brother's neck, taking his life away, with his hand in his pocket, that his smirk on his face didn't say, "I'm protected."*
>
> Source: Ben Pickman. "Former NBA Player Stephen Jackson Leads Press Conference in Wake of 'Twin' George Floyd's Death." *Sports Illustrated*, 29 May 2020, si.com. Accessed 3 Aug. 2020.

WHAT'S THE BIG IDEA?

Take a close look at this passage. What connections did Jackson make between Chauvin's actions and his body language? By whom did Jackson think Chauvin felt protected?

CHAPTER TWO

I CAN'T BREATHE

George Perry Floyd Jr. was born on October 14, 1973, in Fayetteville, North Carolina. His mother, Larcenia Jones Floyd, was a single parent. She moved to Houston, Texas, when George was two years old. They made their new home in the Cuney Homes public housing project. Locals called the complex "The Bricks." It was located in one of the poorest neighborhoods of the city.

George had big dreams. In second grade, he wrote that he wanted to be a

Supporters created a mural and memorial for George Floyd across from Cuney Homes, where he grew up.

Supreme Court Justice when he grew up. By the time he entered Jack Yates High School, his dreams had shifted. He wanted to play professional basketball. He earned a basketball scholarship to South Florida State College. But he ended up disliking Florida. He returned to Texas less than a year later.

LIFE-CHANGING EVENTS

Back in Houston, Floyd got into some trouble with the law. In 2009, he pleaded guilty to aggravated robbery with a deadly weapon. He served four years in prison. After his release, he began doing volunteer work through Resurrection Houston. This was a church near Cuney Homes. He wanted to give back to the community where he grew up.

In 2014 he decided to make a fresh start. He moved to Minneapolis, Minnesota. He got a job as a bouncer at Conga Latin Bistro. It was a good match for Floyd, who stood 6 feet, 7 inches (2 m) tall. His friends had

Minneapolis is the largest city in Minnesota.

OTHER DEATHS INVOLVING MINNESOTA POLICE

Floyd died in the custody of Minnesota police. But his death was not the first in Minnesota to make headlines. In 2015 Jamar Clark was shot in the head during a struggle with Minneapolis police. He died two days later. The officers involved were not disciplined or charged.

In 2016 Philando Castile was pulled over by an officer outside Saint Paul, Minnesota. Castile's girlfriend, Diamond Reynolds, was in the car with her daughter. Officer Jeronimo Yanez shot Castile multiple times. Yanez thought Castile was reaching for a gun. Reynolds said he was reaching for his license. Reynolds broadcast what happened on Facebook Live. Yanez was fired but acquitted of charges.

long looked to him to break up fights with others. They said he had a calming personality. Many of them described him as a gentle giant. During the COVID-19 pandemic in 2020, the nightclub was forced to close.

On Memorial Day, Floyd stopped at a grocery store to buy cigarettes. When he paid for them, the store's employees suspected he had used a counterfeit $20 bill. They called the police.

Floyd died in police custody outside Cup Foods after being suspected of using a counterfeit bill. People created memorials at the store to honor Floyd's memory.

Officers Lane and Kueng arrived a short time later. They arrested Floyd and walked him to their squad car. Floyd began to panic. He explained to the officers that he was claustrophobic. The officers tried to force him into the car.

Then Chauvin and Thao pulled up to the scene. The officers again tried to force Floyd into the car. Floyd repeatedly said that he could not breathe.

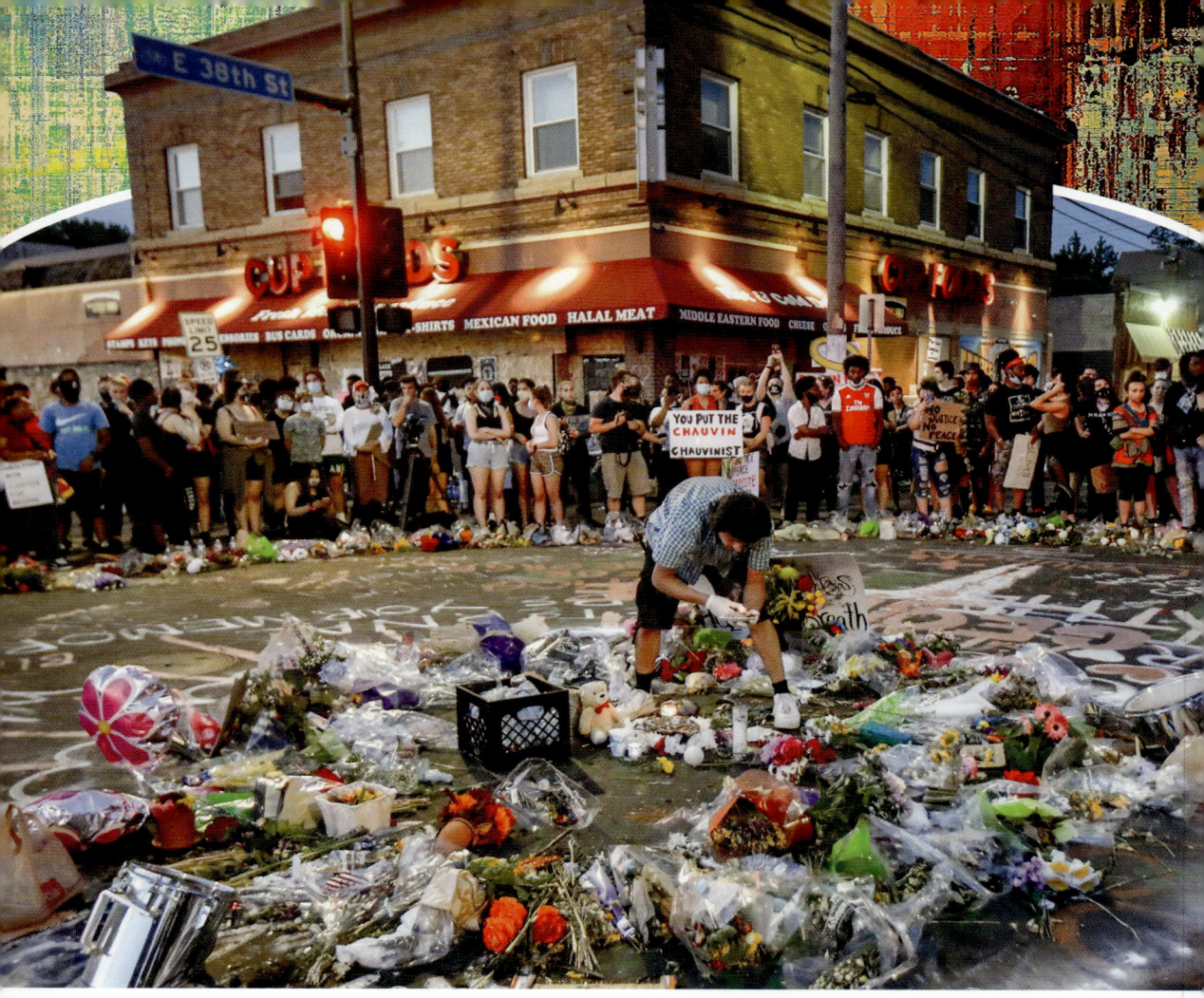

Cup Foods became a focal point for many memorials and protests for Floyd.

Officers pulled Floyd from the car and forced him to the ground. He was still in handcuffs. Chauvin began pressing his knee against Floyd's neck. Kueng knelt on Floyd's back. Lane knelt on Floyd's legs. Floyd begged Chauvin to stop. "I can't breathe," Floyd said more than

20 times. Floyd cried out for his mother. Lane asked Chauvin if they should roll Floyd onto his side. At one point, Kueng checked Floyd's pulse. He told the others he could not find one. But none of the three officers took any action to stop Chauvin. Chauvin held Floyd down even after Floyd became unresponsive. Chauvin kept his knee on Floyd's neck for more than eight minutes.

Strangers who gathered on Chicago

PERSPECTIVES
CHOKE HOLDS AND STRANGLEHOLDS

Some police departments in the United States have banned choke holds and strangleholds. Choke holds apply pressure at the front of a person's neck. Strangleholds apply pressure to the side of the neck. Chauvin used a stranglehold on Floyd. These types of restraints restrict blood flow to a person's brain. Lorenzo Boyd is the Director of the Center for Advanced Policing at the University of New Haven in Connecticut. He explained the danger of choke holds in an interview. "The bottom line is that you're cutting off somebody's air supply," he said. Minneapolis banned choke holds following Floyd's death. Many people think these restraints should be banned at the federal level.

Thanks to the rise of smartphones, many people are always carrying cameras and video cameras. This means people can record events as they happen, including acts of police brutality.

Avenue recorded what was happening with their smartphones. Videos of the incident soon went viral on the internet. Lane, Kueng, and Thao wore body cameras. These cameras recorded what happened during Floyd's arrest. But the footage was not released to the public until August. By then, smartphone videos had already led to public outcry. The body camera footage provided important details about what happened.

A decade earlier, many people did not carry smartphones. It was harder to take videos on short notice. But the video evidence of Floyd's death helped public outrage spread quickly. People demanded that the police officers be held accountable for their actions.

FURTHER EVIDENCE

Chapter Two discusses the video recordings of Floyd's death. What was one of this chapter's main points? What evidence is included to support this point? Read the article at the website below. Does the information on the website support this point? Does it present new evidence?

SMART PHONE VIDEO SHOWS THE FACTS ABOUT AMERICA'S POLICE

abdocorelibrary.com/justice-for-george-floyd

CHAPTER THREE

REMEMBERING GEORGE FLOYD

In the days and weeks following Floyd's death, people across the United States reacted. What began as a single protest in Minneapolis grew into a national movement. People protested police brutality and systemic racism. Protests took place in all 50 states. Groups even gathered in other countries to show their support. They marched for Floyd and others who had died during encounters with police.

Protests against police violence spread to the entire United States. Many protests were held in New York City.

The majority of protests remained peaceful. But some turned destructive and violent. In some cities protesters set police cars and buildings on fire. Many Americans disapproved of these behaviors. Former president Barack Obama was one. He instead urged people to vote for officials who would fight racism. Others thought that the police were directly at fault for the rioting. Professor Clifford Stott is an expert in public order policing at Keele University. During an interview with the BBC, he stated that riots are often a result of the way police treat crowds. For example, in numerous cities police used violence to break up protests. Police used tear gas, rubber bullets, stun guns, or tasers. Tear gas causes severe eye and lung irritation. Stun guns and tasers use electrical charges to immobilize people.

Floyd's death greatly increased support for the Black Lives Matter movement. This organization aims to stop violence against Black people. It was founded in 2013 after the acquittal of George Zimmerman. This armed citizen killed an unarmed Black teen named

PROTESTS ACROSS THE
UNITED STATES

Although the protests against George Floyd's death began in Minneapolis, they quickly spread around the United States. This map shows the number of cities in each state that held protests in the first three weeks after Floyd's death. What do you notice about the different US regions? How does the map help you understand the spread of the protests?

Trayvon Martin. A jury found Zimmerman not guilty of second-degree murder and manslaughter. Since Black Lives Matter was formed, the phrase has become a rallying cry. It helps draw public attention to the deaths of unarmed Black people such as Eric Garner, Jordan Edwards, and many more. But none of these deaths have captured the world's attention as strongly as George Floyd's.

Floyd's death sparked a global conversation about police reform. Many people think the best way to combat systemic racism in police departments is by restructuring the system. They want racist cops removed

LACK OF DIVERSITY

In 2018, 12.8 percent of police officers in the United States were Black. Even fewer held leadership positions within their departments. RaShall Brackney is the chief of police in Charlottesville, Virginia. She did an interview with ABC News amidst the protests of Floyd's death. She pointed out that more Black officers need to be in positions of power if police reform is going to be successful.

from departments. They also want policies that unfairly target Black people to be removed.

FLOYD LAID TO REST IN TEXAS

Thousands of people mourned George Floyd at a public memorial. It was held in Houston on June 8, 2020. Texas governor Greg Abbott joined Houston mayor Sylvester Turner in visiting Floyd's casket. People who knew and loved Floyd were joined by strangers in a long line to enter

PERSPECTIVES
DISBANDING POLICE DEPARTMENTS

Some protesters think police reform will not do enough. They want police departments to be disbanded. Money previously used for police departments would be used for new programs. These programs would focus on housing, mental health, and education. Activists say investing money in these areas would help prevent crime. In June 2020, nine Minneapolis City Council members pledged to disband the city's police department. But council members disagreed about what that would mean. The measure would have to be approved by a committee and then voted on by the public. Many people opposed the idea. It would take time to make significant changes.

Reverend Al Sharpton spoke at Floyd's funeral. Presidential candidate Joe Biden spoke by video, and R&B artist Ne-Yo sang at the funeral.

the church. Only 15 people were allowed inside at a time due to the ongoing pandemic. Each person had to wear a mask. But neither the virus nor the long wait prevented mourners from showing up. They all wanted to pay their respects to Floyd.

Reverend Al Sharpton spoke at the funeral the next day. He described Floyd as having a central role in a movement that will change the world. During the funeral, Sharpton spoke to Floyd directly. He told Floyd that his neck had become a symbol for the suffering of Black people. He assured Floyd that his country would not forget his name.

EXPLORE ONLINE

Chapter Three discusses how people around the world protested the death of George Floyd. How is the information from the article the same as the information in Chapter Three? What new information did you learn from the article?

WHY THE GEORGE FLOYD PROTESTS WENT GLOBAL

abdocorelibrary.com/justice-for-george-floyd

CHAPTER FOUR

A MAN WHO MADE A DIFFERENCE

George Floyd's death caused a wave of activism. Americans responded with anger, frustration, and sadness. People of all backgrounds came together. They protested what they felt were needless killings of Black people by police officers. Taking to the streets, they raised their voices. Their urgency matched the nation's civil rights movement of the 1950s and 1960s. This period of history included numerous protests against racism and discrimination.

The March on Washington was an important protest during the civil rights movement. On its anniversary in 2020, protesters demonstrated against police brutality in the same spot.

33

PERSPECTIVES

KNEELING IN PROTEST

In 2016 San Francisco 49ers quarterback Colin Kaepernick and several other NFL players began kneeling during the national anthem. They did this to protest police brutality against Black people. At that time, the NFL issued a statement encouraging all players to stand during the anthem. But George Floyd's death brought this issue back into the spotlight. NFL commissioner Roger Goodell spoke out in support of kneeling. He said, "We, the National Football League, admit we were wrong for not listening to the NFL players earlier and encourage all to speak out and peacefully protest."

Support for George Floyd was seen in communities that had never been part of a Black Lives Matter event. From big cities to small towns, Americans gathered to demand change. People of all races, ages, and genders joined together. In some cities, police officers expressed their support as well. Some officers even knelt with or joined protesters.

CHARGES FILED AND UPGRADED

The protests put pressure on the Minneapolis Police Department. The public demanded it hold all the officers accountable for their actions. Chauvin was arrested on May 29. He was charged with third-degree murder and second-degree manslaughter. On June 3 the three other officers were arrested. Kueng, Lane, and Thao were charged with aiding and abetting. This means helping another person commit a crime.

Lawyers for Kueng and Lane opposed the charges. Kueng and Lane were rookies. Chauvin was a training officer. The lawyers said Kueng and Lane were following orders. In some police departments, people who speak out against other officers are punished. Other officers may shun them. They may refuse to work with them. This makes officers' jobs harder. But the MPD has a "duty to intervene" policy. This means officers must act if another officer is doing something wrong. Kueng, Lane, and Thao did not stop Chauvin. The charges

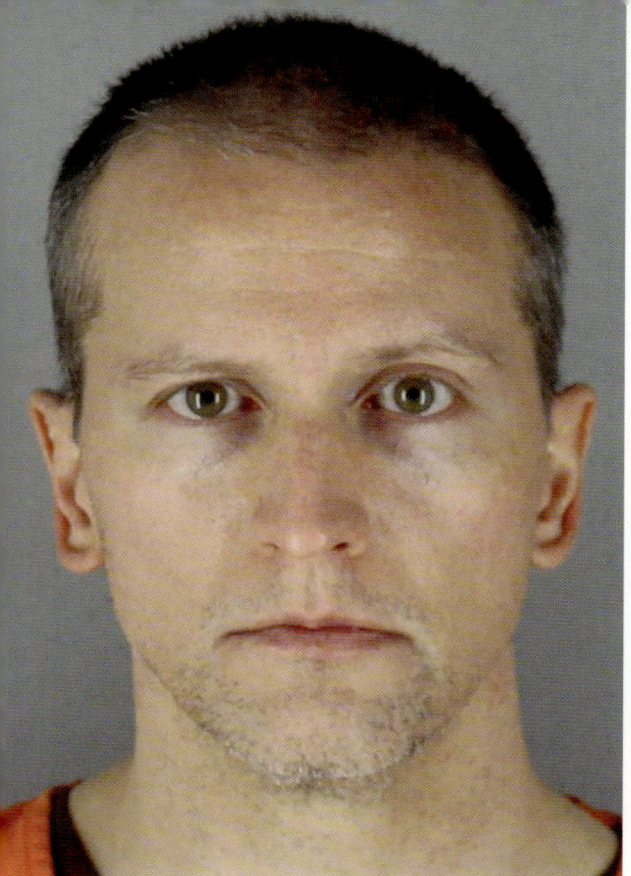 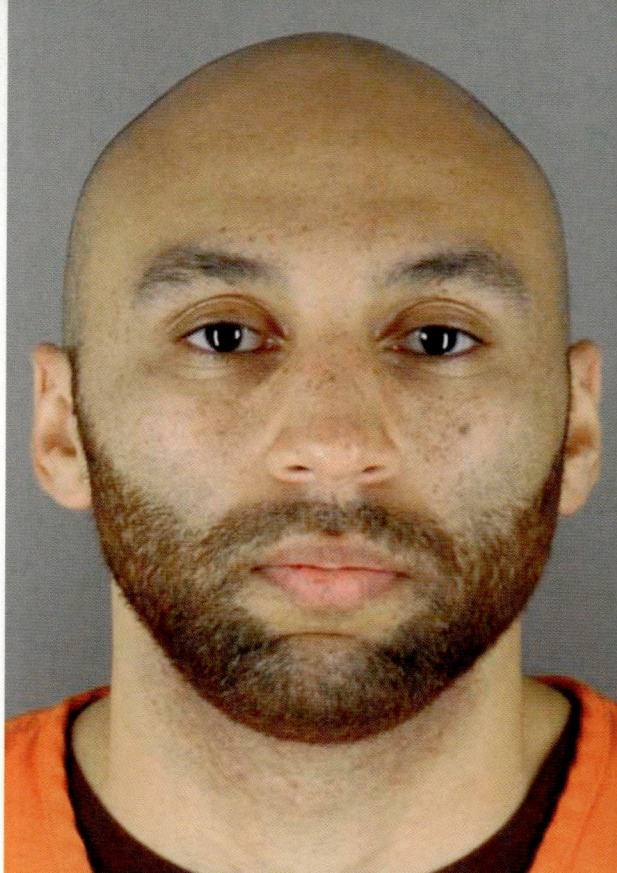

Chauvin, *left*, was charged with murder for the death of George Floyd. Kueng, Lane, and Thao, *second from left to right*, were charged with aiding and abetting.

were a huge victory for the people who had been demanding justice.

Minnesota attorney general Keith Ellison also raised the charges against Chauvin. He raised them from third-degree murder to second-degree murder. Third-degree murder means that there was no intent to harm the victim. Second-degree murder, however, means that harm was the intent, but there was no intent to kill. The higher charge increased the amount of time Chauvin could spend in prison to 40 years. In October, the third-degree charge was dropped.

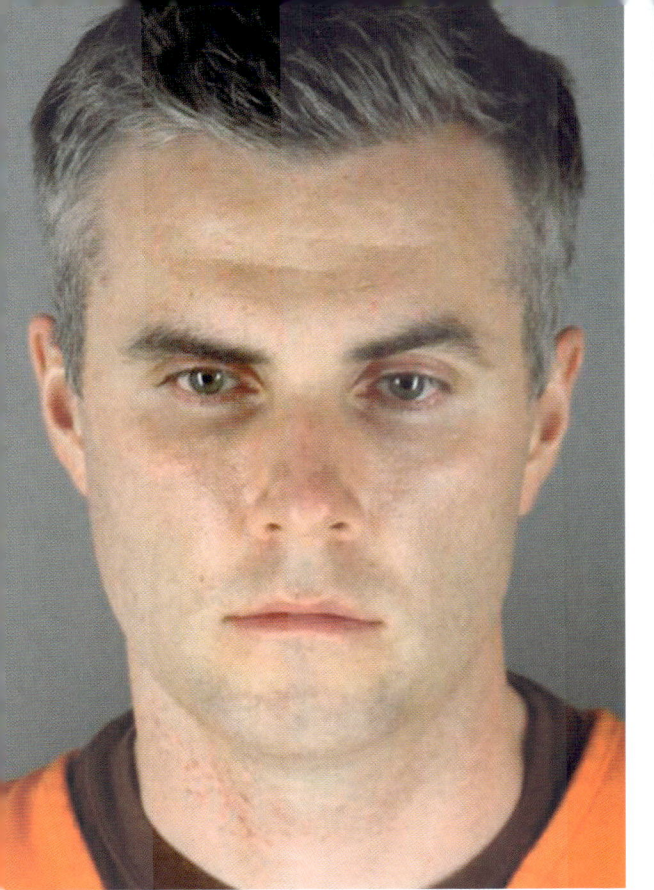

Two autopsies would provide important evidence in the trial. One was performed by the Hennepin County

Medical Examiner. The other was a private autopsy done by the family. The two autopsies found different causes of Floyd's death. The private autopsy said Floyd died because he could not breathe. The county autopsy said Floyd died because his heart stopped. Both autopsies declared Floyd's death a homicide. This means his death was caused by another person.

MAKING REFORM HAPPEN

People raised their voices to call for police reform. The US House of Representatives and Senate responded. Two bills were introduced in the weeks following Floyd's death. House Democrats put forth the George Floyd Justice in Policing Act. Senate Republicans crafted a different bill. It was the Just and Unifying Solutions To Invigorate Communities Everywhere Act of 2020, or JUSTICE Act. Both bills included the creation of a national database. The database would keep track of use-of-force incidents. This would give police departments more knowledge of officers' job histories before hiring them.

However, there were differences between the bills. The George Floyd Justice in Policing Act included a ban on racial profiling. This means banning the use of race instead of behavior as a reason to suspect someone of a crime. It also required the use of police body cameras. The JUSTICE Act did not include these items. The JUSTICE Act would provide funding for departments to buy body cameras. It encouraged the use of

BODY CAMERA POLICIES

Many police departments already use body cameras. The purpose of these devices is to record everything that takes place while an officer is working. Most Americans support using body cameras. But officers can turn off their cameras. Some police departments have also refused to release body camera video following an incident. Different police departments have different policies about the cameras. According to the American Civil Liberties Union, body cameras cannot be effective until their use becomes mandatory. It says the policies about cameras are as important as the cameras themselves.

Murals memorializing George Floyd appeared all over the country and world.

body cameras. But it did not require them. Politicians would need to work together to construct a bill that would satisfy both parties.

George Floyd's death captured the world's attention. It inspired people everywhere to stand up and speak out against the injustices Black people have suffered. True change will take both time and effort. But the momentum of the movement is helping people fight against systemic racism and police brutality.

STRAIGHT TO THE SOURCE

In June 2020 the *New York Times* asked teenagers to share their thoughts about the George Floyd protests. Philadelphia, Pennsylvania, student Jayden Vance's response appeared in the piece:

The protests in [George Floyd's] city spread to cities all across the country because people of all races, religions, and sexualities have had enough of the racism and discrimination against Black people. People have had enough and are finally standing up against the cops. My parents and I are planning to attend protests this week because as a Black person and a Black family, we feel as though it is our responsibility to be a part of this movement.

Source: The Learning Network. "What Students Are Saying about the George Floyd Protests." *New York Times*, 4 June 2020, nytimes.com. Accessed 28 July 2020.

CHANGING MINDS

Imagine you are taking part in a protest for racial justice. What words would you write on the sign you carry? What might you shout to onlookers as you march? How do you feel these words could make a difference? Make sure to explain your opinion. Include facts and details that support your reasons.

IMPORTANT DATES

2014
George Floyd moves to Minnesota, where he hopes to make a fresh start.

May 25, 2020
George Floyd dies in the custody of the Minneapolis Police Department after Officer Derek Chauvin kneels on his neck for more than eight minutes.

May 26, 2020
Chauvin and the three other officers at the scene of Floyd's death are fired. A large protest against Floyd's death takes place in Minneapolis. It is the first of many around the nation and the world.

May 29, 2020
Chauvin is arrested and charged with third-degree murder and second-degree manslaughter.

June 3, 2020
J. Alexander Kueng, Thomas Lane, and Tou Thao are arrested for aiding and abetting. Charges against Chauvin are upgraded to second-degree murder.

June 8, 2020
Thousands of mourners stand in line to pay their respects to George Floyd before his funeral the next day.

STOP AND
THINK

Dig Deeper

After reading this book, what questions do you still have about George Floyd? With an adult's help, find a few reliable sources that can help you answer your questions. Write a paragraph about what you learned.

You Are There

This book discusses the first protest against George Floyd's death in Minnesota. Imagine that you witnessed this protest in person. Write a letter to a friend about this experience. Be sure to add plenty of details to your letter.

Take a Stand

The George Floyd Justice in Policing Act requires all police officers to wear body cameras. The JUSTICE Act encourages body cameras but does not require them. Sometimes officers turn off their body cameras or refuse to submit footage as evidence. Do you think body cameras should be required for all police officers? Why or why not?

GLOSSARY

acquit
to find not guilty of criminal charges

aggravated robbery
a theft in which the victim is injured or threatened by the use of or display of a weapon

autopsy
an examination done after a person dies to determine the cause of death

counterfeit
an item made to imitate something of value

disband
to break up a group or organization

excessive force
action that goes beyond what is necessary

manslaughter
the crime of killing another human being without meaning to cause harm and without planning it in advance

no-knock warrant
a search warrant allowing police to enter a building without saying who they are

wanton endangerment
acting in a way that creates the danger of serious injury or death for another person

ONLINE RESOURCES

To learn more about George Floyd, visit our free resource websites below.

Core Library CONNECTION
FREE! COMMON CORE MULTIMEDIA RESOURCES

Visit **abdocorelibrary.com** or scan this QR code for free Common Core resources for teachers and students, including vetted activities, multimedia, and booklinks, for deeper subject comprehension.

Booklinks NONFICTION NETWORK
FREE! ONLINE NONFICTION RESOURCES

Visit **abdobooklinks.com** or scan this QR code for free additional online weblinks for further learning. These links are routinely monitored and updated to provide the most current information available.

LEARN MORE

Harris, Duchess. *Black Lives Matter*. Abdo Publishing, 2018.

Thomas, Rachael L. *#BlackLivesMatter: Protesting Racism*. Abdo Publishing, 2019.

ABOUT THE AUTHORS

Duchess Harris, JD, PhD

Dr. Harris is a professor of American Studies and Political Science at Macalester College and curator of the Duchess Harris Collection of ABDO books. She is also the coauthor of the collection, which features popular titles such as *Hidden Human Computers: The Black Women of NASA* and series including Freedom's Promise and Race and American Law. In addition, Dr. Harris hosts the Freedom's Promise podcast with her son.

Before working with ABDO, Dr. Harris authored several other books on the topics of race, culture, and American history. She served as an associate editor for *Litigation News*, the American Bar Association Section of Litigation's quarterly flagship publication, and was the first editor in chief of *Law Raza*, an interactive online journal covering race and the law, published at William Mitchell College of Law. She has earned a BA in History from the University of Pennsylvania, a PhD in American Studies from the University of Minnesota, and a JD from William Mitchell College of Law.

Tammy Gagne

Tammy Gagne has written dozens of books for both adults and children. Her recent titles include *The History of Racism in America* and *Race and the Media in Modern America*. She lives in northern New England with her husband and son.

INDEX

Abbott, Greg, 29

Black Lives Matter, 26–28, 34
body cameras, 10, 22–23, 39–40
Boyd, Lorenzo, 21
Brackney, RaShall, 28

Castile, Philando, 18
Chauvin, Derek, 6–8, 13, 19–21, 35–37
Clark, Jamar, 18
Cosgrove, Myles, 12
COVID-19 pandemic, 5, 18, 30
Cuney Homes, 15–16
Cunningham, Phillipe, 29

Edwards, Jordan, 10, 28
Ellison, Keith, 36

Floyd, Larcenia Jones, 15, 21
Freeman, Mike, 8
Frey, Jacob, 8

Garner, Eric, 10, 28
George Floyd Justice in Policing Act, 38–40
Goodell, Rodger, 34

Hankison, Brett, 12

Jackson, Stephen, 13
JUSTICE Act, 38–40

Kaepernick, Colin, 34
Kueng, J. Alexander, 7, 19–22, 35

Lane, Thomas, 7, 19–22, 35

Martin, Trayvon, 26–28
Mattingly, Jon, 12
Minneapolis Police Department, 7, 18, 21, 29, 35

Obama, Barack, 26
Oliver, Roy, 10

Pantaleo, Daniel, 10
protests, 5–6, 8, 25–28, 33–35, 40, 41

Reynolds, Diamond, 18

Sharpton, Al, 31
Stott, Clifford, 26
systemic racism, 12, 25, 28, 40

Taylor, Breonna, 10–12
Thao, Tou, 7, 19, 22, 35
Turner, Sylvester, 29

Vance, Jaydan, 41

Walker, Kenneth, 11–12

Yanez, Jeronimo, 18

Zimmerman, George, 26–28